WEARING
BRACES

BY HARRIET BRUNDLE

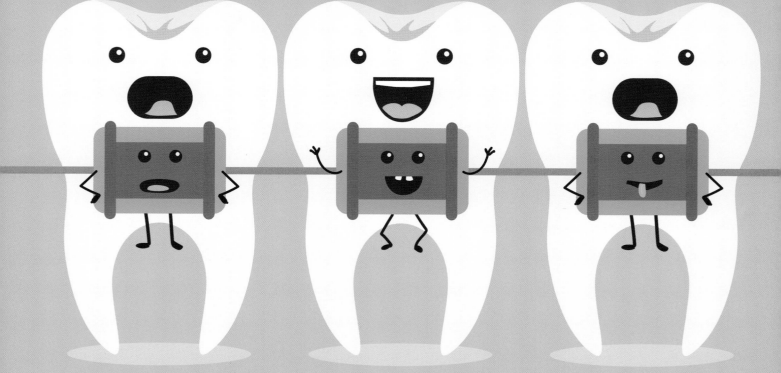

KidHaven
PUBLISHING

HUMAN BODY HELPERS

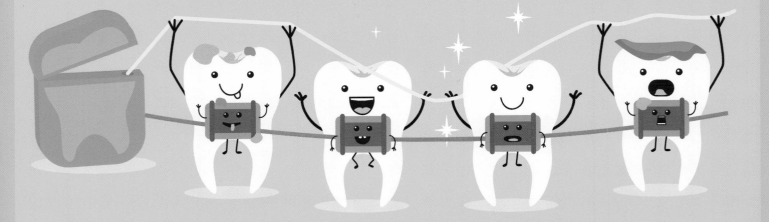

Published in 2019 by
KidHaven Publishing, an Imprint of Greenhaven Publishing, LLC
353 3rd Avenue
Suite 255
New York, NY 10010

Designer: Danielle Rippengill
Editor: Kirsty Holmes

Photo credits: *All images are courtesy of Shutterstock.com, unless
otherwise specified. With thanks to Getty Images, Thinkstock Photo and
iStockphoto. Front Cover & 1 – grmarc, Beatriz Gascon J, NikaMooni,
Milan M. Images used on every spread – grmarc, Beatriz Gascon J,
NikaMooni, yana shypova. 2 – EstherQueen999. 5 – Puslatronik. 7 –
Paladjai. 8 – Puslatronik. 9 – nedofedo. 10 & 11 – Paladjai. 12 – JK's Design.
14 & 16 – EstherQueen999. 18 – Irina Strelnikova, SIMPILI. 19 & 20 –
EstherQueen999. 22 & 23 – EstherQueen999.*

All facts, statistics, web addresses and URLs in this book were verified
as valid and accurate at time of writing. No responsibility for any
changes to external websites or references can be accepted by either
the author or publisher.

Cataloging-in-Publication Data

Names: Brundle, Harriet.
Title: Wearing braces / Harriet Brundle.
Description: New York : KidHaven Publishing, 2019. | Series: Human
body helpers | Includes glossary and index.
Identifiers: ISBN 9781534529434 (pbk.) | ISBN 9781534529458 (library
bound) | ISBN 9781534529441 (6 pack) | ISBN 9781534529465
(ebook)
Subjects: LCSH: Orthodontics–Juvenile literature. | Orthodontic
appliances–Juvenile literature. | Teeth–Juvenile literature.
Classification: LCC RK521.B77 2019 | DDC 617.643–dc23

Printed in the United States of America

CPSIA compliance information: Batch #BW19KL: For further information contact Greenhaven
Publishing LLC, New York, New York at 1-844-317-7404.

Please visit our website, www.greenhavenpublishing.com. For a free
color catalog of all our high-quality books, call toll free 1-844-317-7404
or fax 1-844-317-7405.

CONTENTS

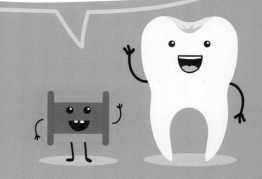

Words that look like **this** can be found in the glossary on page 24.

YOUR TEETH

TEETH ... WE ALL HAVE THEM. BUT WHY DO WE NEED THEM?

Your teeth help you chew, bite, and tear food so that you can swallow it. They also help you to **pronounce** words and sounds.

Hi! I'm Millie Molar and I'm one of your teeth. I've got the job of chewing up and grinding your food.

The top part of a tooth is called the crown and that's the part you can see.

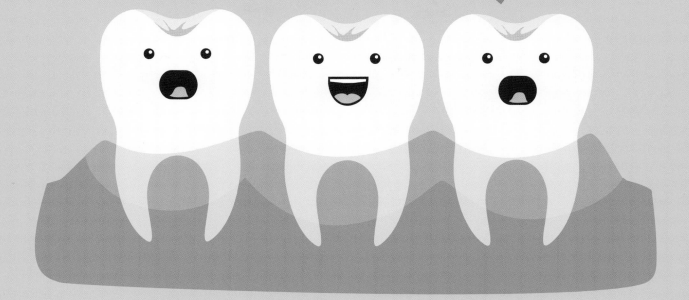

The roots of your teeth are under your gums and keep your teeth in position.

It's really important you look after us because once your **permanent** teeth have come through, we're yours for the rest of your life!

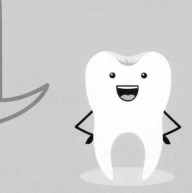

WHAT ARE BRACES?

BRACES ARE USED TO STRAIGHTEN OR CORRECT TEETH.

Fixed braces have brackets that are **bonded** to your teeth with wires joining them together.

I'm Bertie Bracket. I'm one part of a set of fixed braces and I'll be sticking around for a while!

There are also removable braces and **retainers**.
These can be taken out while eating or to be cleaned.

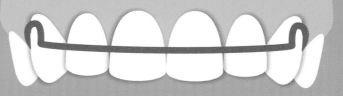

REMOVABLE ESSIX RETAINER

HAWLEY RETAINER

I usually spend between 12 and 24 months on your teeth.

Removable braces can only do their job if they are worn for the correct amount of time.

WHY MIGHT I NEED BRACES?

You might need braces because your teeth are crooked, have too much space between them, or are **overcrowded**. Braces will correct your teeth so you can eat and talk as you should.

When your adult teeth come through, we don't always come through correctly. That's where braces help out!

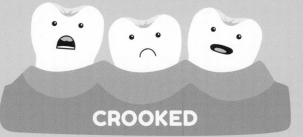

CROOKED

OVERCROWDED

SPACE

Once we've finished our job of correcting your teeth, it can make them easier to care for, too.

YOU MIGHT NEED BRACES BECAUSE YOUR BOTTOM TEETH OVERLAP YOUR TOP TEETH OR THE OTHER WAY AROUND.

When your upper teeth overlap your bottom teeth too much, it's called an overbite.

The other way around is called an underbite.

HOW DO BRACES WORK?

FIXED BRACES ARE MADE UP OF BRACKETS AND AN <u>ARCHWIRE</u>.

Each bracket has a slot for the archwire to go through.

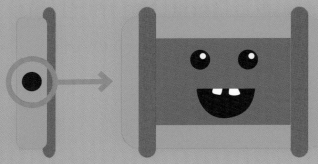

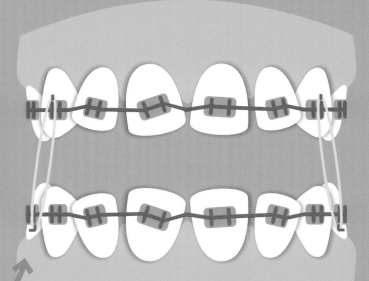

Some fixed braces also have parts called alastics to hold the wire in place.

Usually, you can pick the color of the alastics! Mine are blue.

The archwire puts **pressure** on the brackets, which in turn put pressure on our teeth.

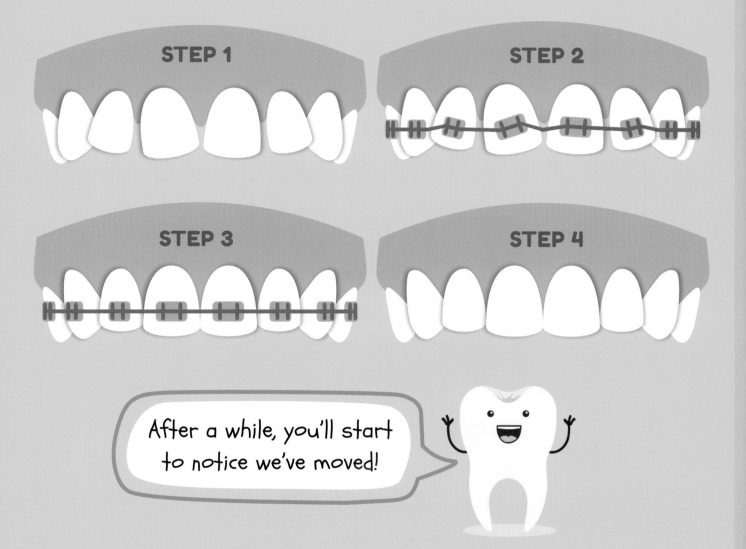

As this happens over a long period of time, your teeth begin to move in the direction your braces want them to go.

WHAT HAPPENS AT THE ORTHODONTIST?

Once you know you need braces, your **orthodontist** will usually take some X-rays of your teeth and make some **molds**.

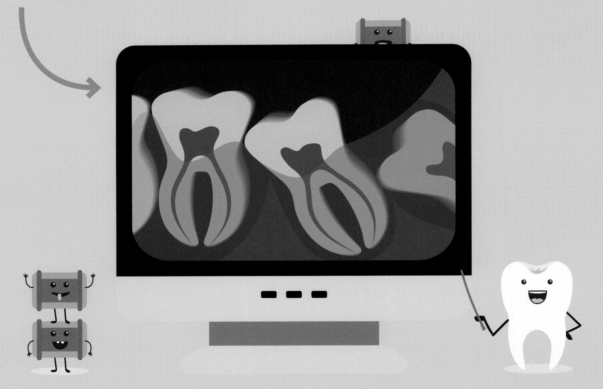

This is done so that they can plan exactly what they need to do to make your braces work best for you.

Before the orthodontist puts your braces on, your teeth are usually cleaned and then dried. The orthodontist will use glue to stick each of the brackets to your teeth, then put the archwire in the brackets and secure it with alastic ties.

Hi! I'm Millie Molar! It's lovely to meet you.

Hi! I'm Bertie Bracket. I'm part of your new braces.

WHAT TO EXPECT

WHILE YOUR BRACES ARE BEING PUT ON, IT SHOULDN'T BE PAINFUL.
Your mouth might feel a bit strange to start with, while you're getting used to the feeling of having the braces in your mouth.

It won't take long to get used to me, Millie.

STICK BERTIE HERE

In the week after you've had your braces put on, you might feel some discomfort or an aching feeling.

Don't worry, though. After a few weeks you'll be used to having your braces on and the discomfort will go away.

While you're wearing your braces, you'll be going to see your orthodontist **regularly**.

Each time you go, your orthodontist will check your braces to make sure they are not damaged in any way. They will also make sure your teeth are moving as they should.

Each time you go to the orthodontist, they may change your archwire or replace the alastic ties.

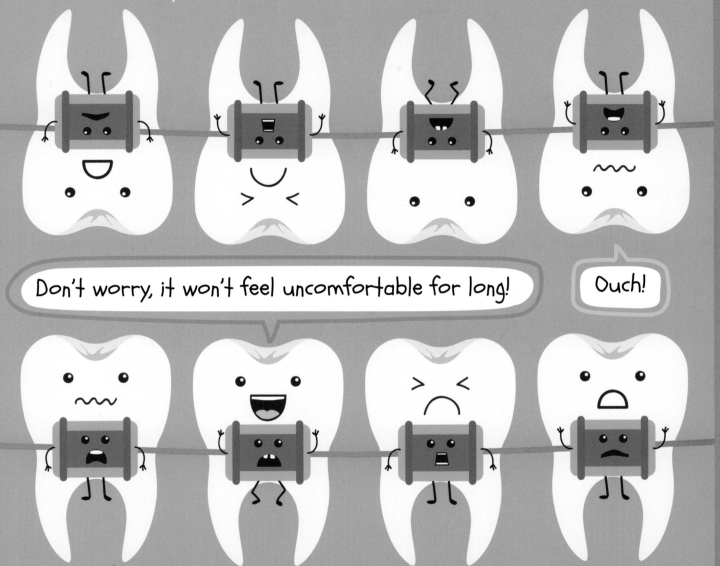

Don't worry, it won't feel uncomfortable for long!

Ouch!

This might make it feel as though there is more pressure on your teeth and that your braces are tighter.

DOS AND DON'TS

DO avoid sticky foods such as chewing gum or caramel, as they can easily get stuck to your braces.

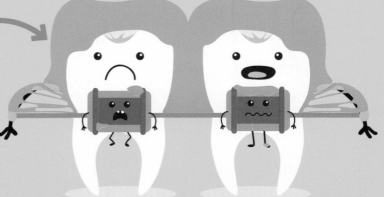

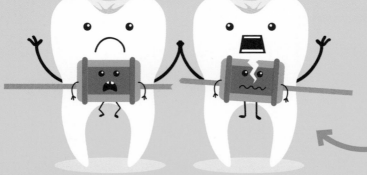

DON'T eat hard or crunchy foods, as they can damage your wire or brackets.

I don't want to be damaged, so if you want something crunchy, like an apple, try cutting it into smaller pieces.

DO try to brush your teeth after every meal if you can and make sure you get a new toothbrush regularly.

While Bertie is here, we need a little extra care and attention.

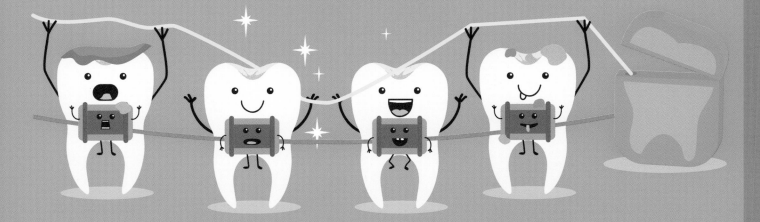

DON'T eat too many sugary foods, like candy, as it could cause **tooth decay** or stain your teeth around the brackets.

BYE BYE BRACES!

ONCE YOUR TEETH ARE WHERE THEY SHOULD BE, YOUR ORTHODONTIST WILL TAKE YOUR BRACES OFF.

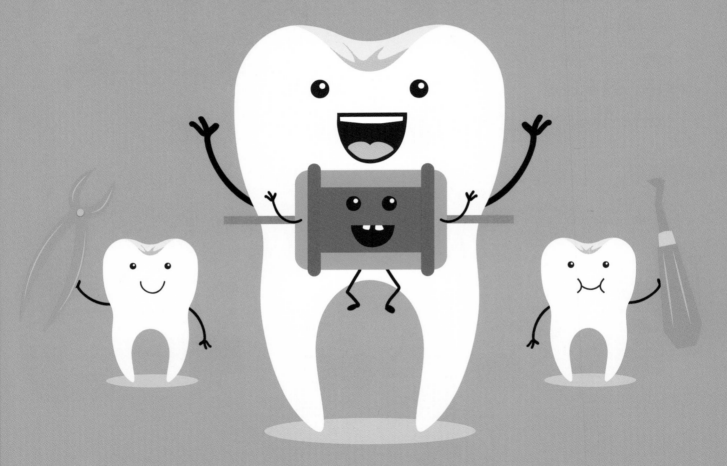

The orthodontist will usually use **pliers** to take off the brackets and then scrape away the glue.

Your mouth might feel a bit strange after your braces have been taken off because you will be so used to it!

Your teeth and gums might feel a bit sore, too, but that feeling will usually go away within a few days.

LIFE AFTER BRACES

YOUR ORTHODONTIST WILL TAKE A MOLD OF YOUR TEETH.

This is for your retainer, which helps to keep your teeth in the correct place after your braces have come off. Your retainer is a type of removable brace.

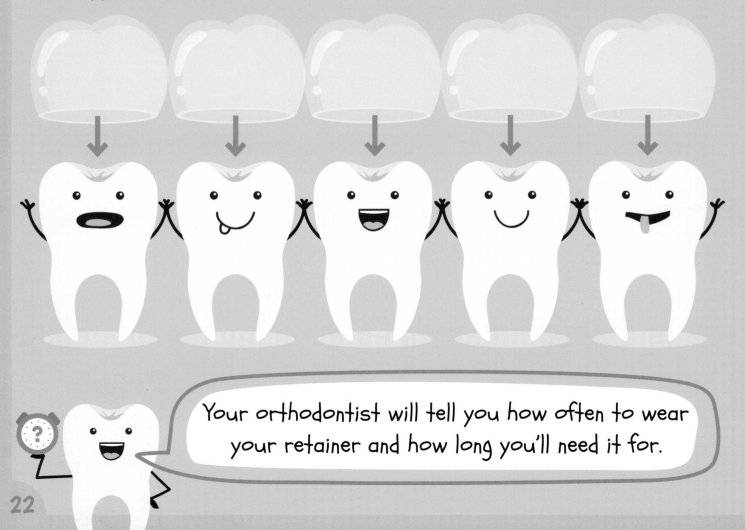

Your orthodontist will tell you how often to wear your retainer and how long you'll need it for.

Now that your braces have come off, your teeth are where they need to be and should now be easier to take care of.

Don't forget to wear your retainer!

Make sure to keep up with brushing twice a day and go to see your orthodontist regularly.

GLOSSARY

ARCHWIRE	a type of wire used by orthodontists to change the position of teeth
BONDED	joined together
MOLDS	imprints made in a malleable material
ORTHODONTIST	a dentist who is trained to treat crooked teeth and fit braces
OVERCROWDED	an amount that is beyond usual or comfortable
PERMANENT	(intended to) last forever
PLIERS	a tool used for gripping or pulling
PRESSURE	a force on or against an object
PRONOUNCE	make a sound in the correct way
REGULARLY	doing something in a constant pattern
RETAINERS	devices used to keep your teeth in place
TOOTH DECAY	when the surface of the tooth breaks down because of plaque

INDEX